Rainbow Smoothies Cookbook

Top 35 Smoothie recipes for Weight Loss, Detox, Cleansing, and a Healthy Diet

Text Copyright © [Anna Bright]

All rights reserved. No part of this guide may be reproduced in any form without permission in writing from the publisher except in the case of brief quotations embodied in critical articles or reviews.

Legal & Disclaimer

The information contained in this book and its contents is not designed to replace or take the place of any form of medical or professional advice; and is not meant to replace the need for independent medical, financial, legal, or other professional advice or services, as may be required. The content and information in this book have been provided for educational and entertainment purposes only.

The content and information contained in this book have been compiled from sources deemed reliable, and it is accurate to the best of the Author's knowledge, information, and belief. However, the Author cannot guarantee its accuracy and validity and cannot be held liable for any errors and/or omissions. Further, changes are periodically made to this book as and when needed. Where appropriate and/or necessary, you must consult a professional (including but not limited to your doctor, attorney, financial advisor or such other professional advisor) before using any of the suggested remedies, techniques, or information in this book.

Upon using the contents and information contained in this book, you agree to hold harmless the Author from and against any damages, costs, and expenses, including any legal fees potentially resulting from the application of any of the information provided by this book. This disclaimer applies to any of the loss, damages or injury caused by the use and application, whether directly or indirectly, of any advice or information presented, whether for breach of contract, tort, negligence, personal injury, criminal intent, or under any other cause of action.

You agree to accept all risks of using the information presented in this book.

You agree that, by continuing to read this book, where appropriate and/or necessary, you shall consult a professional (including but not limited to your doctor, attorney, or financial advisor or such other advisor as needed) before using any of the suggested remedies, techniques, or information in this book.

Table of Contents

Book Description 1

Introduction 4

    Why Choose Rainbow Smoothies? 4

    Advantages Of Rainbow Smoothies 6

    Benefits Of Rainbow Smoothies 7

Basic Rules Of Rainbow Smoothies 8

7 Day-Cleansing Plan 14

    Misconceptions 15

    Dos & Don'ts Of A 7-Day Plan 16

    Build A Road Map To Success By Following Our 7-Day Diet Plan 18

Recipes 23

    5 Red Smoothies 23

        Zesty Beets Smoothie 23

        Red Fruits Smoothie 26

        Scrumptious Red Smoothie 29

        Red Fat-Burning Smoothie 32

        Cherries And Tabasco Smoothie 35

    5 Orange Smoothies 38

        Pumpkin Pie Smoothie 38

Orange Julius 41

Orange And Banana Smoothie 44

Orange Dream Smoothie 47

Weight Loss Smoothie 50

5 Yellow Smoothies 53

Yummy Yellow Smoothie 53

Ultimate Yellow Smoothie 56

Yellow Mellow Smoothie 59

Simple Yellow Smoothie 62

Sunshine Smoothie 65

5 Green Smoothies 67

Go Green Smoothie 67

Scrub Yourself Smoothie 70

Fruit Mix Green Smoothie 73

Electric Green Smoothie 76

Apple Pie Smoothie 79

5 Blue Smoothies 82

Best Blue Smoothie 82

Blue Banana Smoothie 85

Mixed Berries Smoothie 88

Creamy Blue Smoothie 91

Perfect Blue Smoothie 94

5 Light Blue Smoothies 97

Light Blue Smoothie 97

Delicious Smoothie 100
Perfect Light Blue Smoothie 104
Scrumptious Blue Smoothie 107
Blue Banana And Spinach Smoothie 110
5 Purple Smoothies 113
Purple Power Smoothie 113
Purple Punch Smoothie 116
Detox Purple Smoothie 119
Four Ingredients Smoothie 122
Purple Smoothie 125
How To Choose The Best Smoothie Blender, And Cups Or Bottles 128
The Best Smoothie Blenders 128
The Best Smoothie Cups Or Bottles 130
Conclusion 134

BOOK DESCRIPTION

If you are a smoothie lover and you want to travel through the journey to a healthy lifestyle that offers a rainbow of smoothies, then this book is just for you. This smoothie book offers a dozen benefits in a single sip. This book is all about making some delicious, less boring, healthy, organic, green, low caloric, detoxifying, and high protein smoothies, which serve as a magical elixir for your bodies.

If you are obese and want to lose weight, or you are looking for some detox options, or maybe your doctor recommends that you add more fruits and vegetables to your diet, then our rainbow smoothies are the perfect solution for all these issues. Moreover, the smoothies introduced in this book will help you choose perfect meal replacement options. For some people, smoothies are as enjoyable as enjoying dessert. Sure the smoothies help you to satisfy your sweet craving, but they offer more than that. If you are looking for some post- or pre-workout smoothies, then this book will offer some muscle building high protein smoothies that help you to achieve your gym goals.

Unlike some other marketing gambits, our smoothies are healthy, nutritious, organic, appealing, and not dull to the eye, which makes them more appetizing. We are offering red, green, orange, purple, blue, light blue and yellow smoothies. All the smoothies introduced in the book are highly nutritious and designed to keep your brain and body healthy. These smoothies not only help you to add different raw vegetables and fruit to your diet but also satisfy your sweet tooth, in a healthy way. The book incorporates 35 different smoothies divided into seven categories based on color. Thus, you can try a new smoothie every day.

Along with these delicious and beneficial smoothies, we have introduced a full-week diet plan. This diet plan helps you to follow a 3-day diet plan of cleansing and detox. You can choose any 3 days out of the full week, according to your own choice and preference. But for some great results, we recommend that you follow our full 7-day cleansing plan, which helps you detox, lose weight, regain energy, and find your best smoothies.

So, let's jump in for the mouthwatering journey

CHAPTER- 1

Introduction

As implied by the name, this book is targeted toward all those people who want to enjoy a smoothie that is healthy. If you are a person who wants to change your physical appearance, or you want to lose excess weight or reduce inflammation in your body, or you want to flush extra toxins from the blood, then this book is just for you. Our rainbow smoothies serve as a ray of joy. The combinations chosen in this book are so amazing that you will be able to stop worrying over too much caloric intake. But before jumping forward, it's crucial to get a basic understanding of the smoothies.

Why Choose Rainbow Smoothies?

Rainbow Smoothies are considered a very good source for increasing your nutritional intake without breaking the food rules. Including a glass of our rainbow smoothies in your daily menu is a very healthy way to improve brain and body functionality. Our rainbow smoothies are the finest concoctions that include many colorful fresh fruits, vegetables, herbs, protein powder, milk, nuts, and seeds blended to their finest consistency.

Thus, if you find that eating and including vegetables or fruits in your diet is a challenging process, then rainbow smoothies are the solution. For many people, smoothies are the real deal since they consider them as a valuable medical supplement. A lot of the time people having physical conditions such as heart disease, low energy and stamina, weak bones, falling hair, bad skin, vitamin deficiency, and allergies ask their physicians if they would recommend the smoothies diet. Rainbow Smoothies are very easy and quick to make with very little fuss. And in addition, they fill your body with nutrients that serve as health-fighting agents.

Nowadays few of us face the argument whether or not a glass of smoothie can really help overcome these illnesses. In short, yes smoothies can! There are thousands of well-known documentaries and evidence that provide proof that people who adopt smoothie diets are successful in fighting their illnesses. It's all about combinations and ingredient choices that help people move toward their goals effectively and efficiently.

Advantages of Rainbow Smoothies

- The rainbow smoothies are easy and quick to prepare.
- It's one of the best ways to consume your daily portions of vegetables and fruits.
- The rainbow smoothies are full of nutrition and minerals that help improve digestion.
- They strengthen the immune system.
- The rainbow smoothies supply a good amount of energy for your body.
- They help control hunger pangs and reduce cravings for sweets.
- They also help to satisfy the sweet tooth.
- Rainbow smoothies help improve your gallbladder performance.
- They reduce the risk of a heart attack.
- They help in controlling and reducing the risks of high cholesterol.
- They help to improve your mood and make you feel happy.
- Smoothies fill the human body with antioxidants.

Benefits of Rainbow Smoothies

Some of the potential benefits of rainbow smoothies are listed below:

- Shiny and longer hair
- Healthy and flawless skin
- Effective and fast metabolism
- Prevention of illness
- Reduce allergies
- Reduce anxiety, stress, and hypertension
- Cleanse the body by flushing out all the harmful toxins
- Serve as anti-aging aids
- Initiate the weight-loss process
- Control type 2 diabetes

CHAPTER- 2

Basic Rules of Rainbow Smoothies

The smoothie is a delicious way to reach your health goals. If you love the smoothie, then you should also follow the perfect smoothie-making rules to enjoy a wonderful and refreshing drink anytime you like. Every smoothie is created differently because of the combination of different ingredients. So how do you know that the smoothie that you are making is a healthy and perfect blend of nutrients? Here are the few rules that help you to make a perfect smoothie.

Use a Very Healthy Liquid as a Base

Most smoothies are made with some liquid base. These liquids can be fruit juice, milk, or even water. Fruits themselves contain a huge amount of sugar. Therefore, it is better to make a smoothie using an unsweetened liquid-based such as:

Ice

Water

Milk

Yogurt

Greek yogurt

Nut milk

Coconut water

Avoid At-Home Smoothie Kits

We don't recommend the use of any smoothie kits. No doubt a smoothie kit is a great way to save time, but these kits contain cornstarch, gum preservatives, added fruit concentrates, and sugar. All of these lead to a glass of something that is much less healthy and higher in sugar content than the ones made with the recipes in this book.

Use Frozen Items

If you want to make the smoothie quickly, then one tip is to freeze your vegetables and fruits in the refrigerator and use them when you are making a smoothie. This will make your smoothie cold.

Choose Low-Sugar Fruits Whenever You Are Going To Make a Smoothie

Always choose ingredients that are lower in sugar and higher in protein, minerals, fiber, and vitamins. Some of the superfoods are a great way to make a perfect healthy smoothie. Always use moderation when making any kind of smoothie. Addition of extra ingredients is not a great idea. Don't forget to add protein to the smoothie.

Add Protein Powder for Extra Energy

If you make a smoothie that only contains fruit, then it will be very high in carbohydrate and very low in protein and fat. Therefore, we suggest that you always add some kind of protein to your smoothie in the form of nuts, seeds or even protein powder.

Adding protein powder to your smoothies helps make you feel full. It also helps to prevent hunger pangs. Protein powder is a great source of protein.

Add Healthy Fats to the Glass of Smoothie

Fat is a very important nutrient that helps you feel satisfied and makes you feel full for the longest period of time. If you eliminate fat from your diet, then your body will not feel satisfied, and you will always be feeling hungry. Try to add a good source of fat to your glass in the form of avocados, flax seeds, chia seeds, and nut oils.

Including such fats in your smoothie gives you countless benefits, since all of these ingredients are rich in minerals and antioxidants, which help cleanse and detoxify your body. The chia seeds and flax seeds contain Omega-3 and those fatty acids that have an anti-inflammatory effect on the body.

Add Some Fiber

Fiber is very important and beneficial to the human body. It slows down the movement of food from the stomach to the intestine. The fiber slows down the digestive process and helps the body absorb all the nutrients from the food. It decreases the number of calories and lowers the blood glucose level after a meal. Adding fiber to your smoothie helps you to maintain healthy bowel movements. It lowers the cholesterol and keeps the colon cells healthy. The fiber in the smoothie can be added in the form of raspberries, almonds, pistachios, coconut flakes, and seeds.

Forget the Added Sweeteners

As we stressed earlier, fruits are a great source of natural sugar and glucose that are enough to satisfy your craving for sweet. So whenever you are making a smoothie, it is best not to sweeten it. Added natural sugar in the form of honey is acceptable.

Get Creative

There are dozens of healthy ways to help you boost the flavor of the smoothie. You can enhance the flavor of the smoothie by adding ginger, mint leaves, cinnamon, pepper, lime juice, and lemon juice, to name a few.

Myths about Smoothies

Some of the myths that are most common are listed below:

- Smoothies are high in calories.
- Smoothies are high in sugar.
- The vitamin intake can be excessive if we drink smoothies regularly.
- Chewing is much better than drinking.
- Smoothies require expensive blenders for the preparation process.
- Blenders destroy enzymes inside the food.
- Smoothies are expensive to prepare.

Your biggest do-over is just a few steps away

CHAPTER- 3

7 Day-Cleansing Plan

This portion of the book includes the basic 7-day diet plan, which includes smoothie recipes that are divided into 7 basic categories. These choices can be adopted, to follow a 3-day diet plan, but we strongly recommend that our readers follow a full 7-day diet plan to get some awesome results.

All these smoothies, when served as a meal replacement, provide energy for workout sessions, help regain lost energy, and also help to initiate weight loss. Before jumping straight to the 7-day plan, it's important to take a glimpse at all the permissible and non- permissible ingredients of rainbow smoothies. There are a lot of misconceptions about what to add and what not to add, what's beneficial or what's not beneficial for the human body.

So, the next part helps clear up some misconceptions about our ingredient choices.

Misconceptions

Nuts Are a Bad Choice and Make Smoothies High In Fat

The nuts are super foods that are the most amazing item that can be included while making any smoothie. Nuts' benefits are countless— most nuts help prevent heart disease and are rich in protein and minerals. Nuts contain fats of a kind that will never make you obese. Almost all of the nut fat and organic nut butter are good for your brain and heart health. And it helps strengthen the body's cells.

Fruits Contain an Excess Amount of Sugar That Can Cause Weight Gain

It's only a misconception since fruits are lower in sugar and contain natural glucose. Moreover, fruits are rich in fiber, protein, calcium, and minerals.

Artificial Sweeteners Are a Good Choice to Add as a Sweetener to the Smoothie

Yes, artificial sweeteners contain almost zero calories and add sweetness to the smoothies, but they are the worst choice one can make, since adding artificial sweeteners only make you crave sweet. They also alter gut bacteria.

Dos & Don'ts Of A 7-Day Plan

Incorporating smoothies into your daily meal plan is a good choice. The smoothies, along with their countless benefits, can also help detox the body. But the most important thing that one needs to know is that the smoothie works very effectively for some people, but for others, it totally fails to deliver results. It is important to look at all the factors that may contribute toward not reaping the rewards from the smoothie diet plan. So if you are one who has decided to follow our 7-day diet plan, then you need to follow some dos and don'ts of the program.

Dos on our 7-Day Diet Plan

The most important step is to replace one of your meals with a rainbow smoothie.

When you are preparing the smoothies, always opt for organic, fresh, and natural items rather than factory packed, canned, or frozen food items.

It's very important to keep track of your weight.

You need to discontinue caffeine and alcohol.

If you feel hungry and have a big appetite, then start with nuts, seeds, or protein powder based smoothies.

Our smoothie program is all about detox, losing weight, and regaining energy, so it's very important to stop all junk food items during the smoothie diet plan. It helps you to reboot your metabolism and digestive system.

If you are just looking for cleansing and detoxifying, then we recommend not to follow a very strict gym regime at the start.

Choose all the nuts, seeds, vegetables, and fruits that suit you.

You can replace the dairy products with low carb non-dairy items if you are lactose intolerant.

Don'ts On the 7-Day Plan

If you are suffering from heart disease, diabetes, or have some other serious chronic health issues, then you should not make these following mistakes: You should not include artificial sweeteners in your smoothie.

Don't be a couch potato.

You should not indulge in eating deep fried items.

Don't add heavy full-fat cream to your smoothies.

Our 7-day diet plan helps you to find balance in the meal plan, and it fulfills all your needs. You can adopt this diet plan according to your daily needs. It supports and enhances your own ability to experience well-being.

Build a Road Map to Success by Following Our 7-Day Diet Plan

Eliminate meat, packaged items, cheese, artificial food, alcohol, and too much caffeine. Go for a very organic and light meal. The best choice is to eat all organic food full of nutrients and that contain no processed items, artificial flavorings, or MSG. Try to cook your meal in olive oil or coconut oil.

Day 1

Breakfast: Enjoy 4 boiled egg whites for breakfast accompanied by an Apple Pie Smoothie.

Lunch: Lunch should include one large bowl of tuna salad (about 5–6 ounces). A glass of Go Green Smoothie should serve as the side dish.

Dinner: Eat small portions and low-calorie food; the choice can be a red rice bowl (about 1½–2 ounces) with vegetable soup (about 6 ounces). End the day with a glass of Electric

Green Smoothie, and then go to sleep 2 hours after having dinner.

Day 2

Breakfast: Start your day with a glass of Blue Banana and Spinach Smoothie for breakfast.

Lunch: For lunch enjoy grilled chicken (about 6 ounces) with 2 cucumbers.

Dinner: Choose a Creamy Blue Smoothie as a dinner option.

Day 3

Breakfast: Start your day with a glass of Zesty Beets Smoothie.

Lunch: Enjoy 1 cup of grilled shrimp with a Scrumptious Red Smoothie.

Dinner: Enjoy 3/4 pound of turkey meatballs with two cups of zucchini noodles. End the day by drinking a Best Blue Smoothie

Day 4

Breakfast: Enjoy 2 ounces of scrambled eggs with a Fruit Mix Green Smoothie.

Lunch: Have one avocado with a Sunshine Smoothie.

Dinner: End the day with a menu offering a Yummy Yellow Smoothie with a large bowl of broccoli and carrot salad with 1 cup of sautéed Bok Choy.

Day 5

Breakfast: Enjoy a Red Fat-Burning Smoothie for breakfast.

Lunch: Enjoy a bowl of vegetable chicken soup.

Dinner: Enjoy a half cup of brown rice with 1 cup of sautéed mushrooms. End the day with a glass of Cherries and Tabasco Smoothie

Day 6

Breakfast: Enjoy 2 bananas with a glass of Pumpkin Pie Smoothie

Lunch: Enjoy 4 grilled chicken legs with a glass of Delicious Blue Smoothie.

Dinner: Enjoy Detox Purple Smoothie as dinner.

Day 7

Breakfast: Enjoy a glass of Yellow Mellow Smoothie.

Lunch: Enjoy 8 ounces of grilled or baked salmon with a drizzle of lemon juice.

Dinner: Enjoy a Purple Punch Smoothie along with 1 grilled chicken breast.

Throughout these 7 days, it is important to avoid idleness and to start a light exercise routine; it can be outdoor cycling, a long walk, or even running a few miles.

Let's Start Blending

CHAPTER- 4

Recipes

5 RED SMOOTHIES

Zesty Beets Smoothie

If you are bored of simple and plain smoothies, then try our red smoothie that provides the boost in energy, and it's a perfect meal replacement option. With a touch of spices, this smoothie provides a zesty punch to your taste buds.

Preparation Time: 5 Minutes

Yield: 4 Servings

Ingredients

- 2 cups of almond milk
- 1½ cups of orange juice
- 1 cup beets, peeled and cubed
- 1 cup of mango chunks, frozen
- 1 cup strawberries, frozen
- ¼ teaspoon lime juice
- Pinch of salt
- Pinch of cayenne pepper

Directions

Add all the smoothie ingredients to the high-speed blender.

Blend at high speed for about 1 minute.

Once smooth in consistency, pour into ice-filled serving glasses and enjoy.

Nutritional Information

Servings: 4

Amount per serving :

Calories 358

% Daily Value

Total Fat 28.9 g 37%

Saturated Fat 25.4 g 127%

Cholesterol 0 mg 0%

Sodium 90 mg 4%

Total Carbohydrate 26.4 g 10%

Dietary Fiber 5.1 g 18%

Total Sugars 19.7 g

Protein 4.1 g

Vitamin D 0 mcg 0%

Calcium 33 mg 3%

Iron 3mg 18%

Potassium 684 mg 15%

Red Fruits Smoothie

This red and tangy drink is the perfect antioxidant punch, which delivers some high-quality properties and nutrients. This smoothie provides a refreshing taste along with detoxification and reduces inflammation.

Preparation Time: 5 Minutes

Yield: 2 Servings

Ingredients

- ¾ cup cranberry juice
- 1 cup strawberry yogurt
- 2 cups strawberries, frozen
- ½ cup raspberries
- 1 teaspoon honey

Directions

Transfer all the smoothie ingredients to a high-speed blender.

Pulse all the ingredients for one minute at high speed.

Once a smooth texture is obtained, pour the smoothie into ice-filled serving glasses.

Serve and enjoy.

Nutritional Information

Servings: 2

Amount per serving:

Calories 216

% Daily Value

Total Fat 2 g 3%

Saturated Fat 0.9 g 5%

Cholesterol 6 mg 2%

Sodium 67 mg 3%

Total Carbohydrate 44.2g 16%

Dietary Fiber 6.4 g 23%

Total Sugars 35.6 g

Protein 6.2 g

Vitamin D 0 mcg 0%

Calcium 207 mg 16%

Iron 1 mg 6%

Potassium 556 mg 12%

Scrumptious Red Smoothie

This delicious and scrumptious smoothie is made with the combination of strawberries, beets, apples, and dates, which make it a perfect anti-inflammatory smoothie. It is a perfect meal replacement option because of some of the superfoods like coconut oil and dates that make it a powerhouse.

Preparation time: 5 minutes

Yield: 2 servings

Ingredients

- 1 small beet, peeled and cubed
- 2 cups of strawberries, fresh
- 1/3 cup of coconut oil, extra virgin
- 4 Medjool dates pitted
- 1 cup of apples, sliced
- 1 cup unsweetened almond milk

Directions

Place all the smoothie ingredients into a high-speed blender.

Process all the ingredients at high speed for 3 minutes.

Once the smoothie is made, serve in tall glasses and enjoy with the addition of ice cubes.

Best served chilled.

Nutritional Information

Servings: 2

Amount per serving :

Calories 739

% Daily Value

Total Fat 38.8 g 50%

Saturated Fat 31.6 g 158%

Cholesterol 0 mg 0%

Sodium 151m g 7%

Total Carbohydrate 104.5g 38%

Dietary Fiber 13.1 g 47%

Total Sugars 80.6 g

Protein 4. 6g

Vitamin D 1 mcg 3%

Calcium 222 mg 17%

Iron 3 mg 15%

Potassium 587 mg 12%

Red Fat-Burning Smoothie

With its own fat-burning powers, this smoothie is perfect for Detox and weight loss.

Preparation Time: 10 Minutes

Yield: 2 Servings

Ingredients

- ½ cup strawberries, fresh
- ¼ cup pistachios

- 1 avocado, peeled, pitted and quartered
- 6 ice cubes, for chilling
- ½ teaspoon vanilla extract
- 4 tablespoons of plant-based protein powder
- 1 cup of water, to blend

Directions

Place all the ingredients in a blender.

Pulse all the ingredients in the blender at high speed for 2 minutes.

Once the smoothie is made, serve it in tall glasses with ice.

Enjoy.

Nutritional Information

Servings: 2

Amount per serving:

Calories 429

% Daily Value

Total Fat 26.3 g 34%

Saturated Fat 5.8 g 29%

Cholesterol 98 mg 33%

Sodium 132 mg 6%

Total Carbohydrate 19.1 g 7%

Dietary Fiber 8.2 g 29%

Total Sugars 4.4 g

Protein 33.3 g

Vitamin D 0 mcg 0%

Calcium 16 4mg 13%

Iron 2 mg 10%

Potassium 832 mg 18%

Cherries and Tabasco Smoothie

The addition of Tabasco makes this recipe full of iron and a very low-calorie smoothie to enjoy. It is a perfect smoothie for weight loss and to boost the metabolism.

Preparation Time: 5 Minutes

Yield: 2 Servings

Ingredients

- 1 cup cherries, pitted
- 1/2 frozen banana
- 1/4 teaspoon of Tabasco sauce
- 1/4 lime
- 1 cup unsweetened almond milk
- 2 tablespoons of plant-based plain protein powder
- 3 ice cubes, for chilling

Directions

Transfer all the smoothie ingredients to a high-speed blender.

Blend at high speed for about two minutes.

Once a smooth texture obtained, pour it into serving glasses and enjoy.

Serve immediately.

Nutritional Information

Servings: 2

Amount per serving:

Calories 204

% Daily Value

Total Fat 3.3 g 4%

Saturated Fat 0. 1g 1%

Cholesterol 0 mg 0%

Sodium 481 mg 21%

Total Carbohydrate 8.2 g 3%

Dietary Fiber 1.3 g 5%

Total Sugars 3.8 g

Protein 38.2 g

Vitamin D 0 mcg 0%

Calcium 455 mg 35%

Iron 14 mg 77%

Potassium 271 mg 6

5 ORANGE SMOOTHIES

Pumpkin Pie Smoothie

It is a creamy, rich, and delicious smoothie, which is full of fiber, protein, minerals, and vitamins. It is a perfect meal replacement smoothie, and it provides instant energy for the body.

Preparation Time: 5 Minutes

Yield: 2 Servings

Ingredients

- 1 cup almond milk, unsweetened
- 2 tablespoons of whey protein powder, vanilla flavor
- 1/3 cup of water
- 1/3 cup canned pumpkin
- 2 teaspoons flaxseed
- 1 teaspoon honey
- 1/4 teaspoon cinnamon
- 1/4 teaspoon vanilla extract
- 1/2 cup of ice cubes, for chilling

Directions

Transfer all the ingredients to a high-speed blender.

Secure the blender lid and blend the ingredients at high speed for 1 minute.

Once a smooth texture is obtained, pour the smoothie into tall serving glasses.

Serve and enjoy.

Nutritional Information

Servings: 2

Amount per serving:

Calories 375

% Daily Value

Total Fat 30.4 g 39%

Saturated Fat 26 g 130%

Cholesterol 32 mg 11%

Sodium 50 mg 2%

Total Carbohydrate 15.7 g 6%

Dietary Fiber 4.6 g 16%

Total Sugars 8.8 g

Protein 14.7 g

Vitamin D 0 mcg 0%

Calcium 85 mg 7%

Iron 4 mg 20%

Potassium 511 mg 11%

Orange Julius

It is a very healthy smoothie that is made from the finest combination of oranges and coconut milk. This smoothie helps lower cholesterol and fight against certain allergies. It is a perfect detoxification smoothie to try.

Preparation Time: 8 Minutes

Yield: 2 Servings

Ingredients

- 4 large oranges, peeled and seeds removed
- 1 cup of ice cubes, for chilling
- 1 cup coconut milk
- 2 tablespoons of honey
- 1 teaspoon of vanilla extract
- 4 ice cubes, for chilling

Directions

Transfer all the smoothie ingredients into a blender.

Blend until smooth in consistency.

Serve and enjoy.

Nutritional Information

Servings: 2

Amount per serving:

Calories 519

% Daily Value

Total Fat 29.1 g 37%

Saturated Fat 25.4 g 127%

Cholesterol 0 mg 0%

Sodium 23 mg 1%

Total Carbohydrate 67.5 g 25%

Dietary Fiber 11.5 g 41%

Total Sugars 55.9 g

Protein 6.3 g

Vitamin D 0 mcg 0%

Calcium 171 mg 13%

Iron 2 mg 14%

Potassium 997 mg 21%

<u>Orange and Banana Smoothie</u>

It is a perfect healthy breakfast smoothie that boosts energy and keeps food cravings at bay for a long time period.

Preparation Time: 10 Minutes

Yield: 2 Servings

Ingredients

- 2 ripe bananas, peeled and frozen
- 1 cup orange juice, fresh
- 1 orange, peeled, seeded and cut into chunks
- ¾ cup almond milk
- 1 teaspoon of vanilla extract
- 1 carrot, peeled and cubed
- 4 ice cubes, for chilling

Directions

Put all the listed ingredients in a high-speed blender.

Blend on high speed until smooth in consistency.

Serve and enjoy.

Nutritional Information

Servings: 2

Amount per serving:

Calories 430

% Daily Value

Total Fat 22.2 g 28%

Saturated Fat 19.2 g 96%

Cholesterol 0 mg 0%

Sodium 37 mg 2%

Total Carbohydrate 58.9 g 21%

Dietary Fiber 8.3 g 30%

Total Sugars 38.2 g

Protein 5.3 g

Vitamin D 0 mcg 0%

Calcium 69 mg 5%

Iron 3 mg 19%

Potassium 1174 mg 25%

Orange Dream Smoothie

Start your metabolic engine with this orange dream smoothie. It not only offers you great taste but also provides metabolism boosting qualities. This scrumptious smoothie is full of vitamin C and helps you shed some extra pounds. It can serve as a perfect breakfast smoothie. It is a filling and energy-boosting smoothie.

Preparation Time: 5 Minutes

Yield: 2 Servings

Ingredients

- 2 oranges, peeled and seeded
- 1 teaspoon vanilla extract
- 2 teaspoons honey
- ½ cup almond milk
- ½ cup Greek yogurt
- 1 cup ice for chilling

Directions

Put the smoothie ingredients, except ice cubes, into a blender and blend ingredients until smooth.

Next, add the ice cubes and blend until ice incorporates well.

Serve in smoothie glasses.

Enjoy.

Nutritional Information

Servings: 2

Amount per serving:

Calories 479

% Daily Value

Total Fat 20.6 g 26%

Saturated Fat 17.3 g 86%

Cholesterol 15 mg 5%

Sodium 108 mg 5%

Total Carbohydrate 43.1 g 16%

Dietary Fiber 5.8 g 21%

Total Sugars 37.3 g

Protein 33.4 g

Vitamin D 0 mcg 0%

Calcium 386 mg 30%

Iron 1 mg 7%

Potassium 921 mg 20%

Weight Loss Smoothie

As the name implies, this smoothie is a perfect weight loss smoothie that not only sheds some extra pounds but also helps to cleanse the digestive system. It is full of fiber and many other essential nutrients.

Preparation Time: 10 Minutes

Yield: 1 Serving

Ingredients

- Pinch of cinnamon
- 2 tablespoons of honey, or to taste
- 1 medium orange, seeds removed and peeled
- Juice of 1 lime
- 1 carrot, peeled and cubed
- 1 tablespoon of flax seed
- ½ cup of water

Directions

Place cinnamon, honey, orange, lime juice, carrot, flax seeds, and water in a blender.

Pulse for about two minutes at high speed.

Once a smooth texture is obtained, pour the smoothie into ice-filled serving glasses.

Serve and enjoy.

Nutritional Information

Servings: 1

Amount per serving:

Calories 244

% Daily Value

Total Fat 2.4 g 3%

Saturated Fat 0.3 g 2%

Cholesterol 0 mg 0%

Sodium 44 mg 2%

Total Carbohydrate 57.6 g 21%

Dietary Fiber 6.7 g 24%

Total Sugars 49.4 g

Protein 3 g

Vitamin D 0 mcg 0%

Calcium 77 mg 6%

Iron 2 mg 13%

Potassium 490 mg 10%

5 YELLOW SMOOTHIES

Yummy Yellow Smoothie

It is an amazing smoothie that is ready in just 5 minutes, and it's full of cleansing properties that help initiate weight loss and clean the toxins from the body. Moreover, it is a gluten-free recipe for you to try.

Preparation Time: 10 Minutes

Yield: 2 Servings

Ingredients

- 1 cup of water
- 1 cup chopped pineapple
- 1 tablespoon of lemon juice
- ½ cucumber, peeled
- 10 dates, pitted
- 4 ice cubes, for chilling

Directions

Put all the ingredients in a blender.

Blend it at high speed, until smooth.

Once the smoothie is prepared, serve in glasses.

Enjoy.

Nutritional Information

Servings: 2

Amount per serving :

Calories 178

% Daily Value

Total Fat 0.4 g 1%

Saturated Fat 0. g 0%

Cholesterol 0 mg 0%

Sodium 4 mg 0%

Total Carbohydrate 47.4 g 17%

Dietary Fiber 5.7 g 20%

Total Sugars 36.4 g

Protein 2.3 g

Vitamin D 0 mcg 0%

Calcium 46 mg 4%

Iron 1 mg 6%

Potassium 513 mg 11%

Ultimate Yellow Smoothie

This smoothie is loaded with antioxidants that help improve skin and vision. The smoothie includes turmeric that has some remarkable inflammation fighting qualities. The addition of pineapple makes it a natural powerhouse that helps the body digest protein.

Preparation Time: 10 Minutes

Yield: 3 Servings

Ingredients

- 2 cups almond milk
- 2 bananas, peeled and frozen
- 1 cup pineapple, frozen
- 1/3 cup yellow squash
- 1/2 teaspoon turmeric
- 1 teaspoon honey
- 1/4 inch of ginger root, peeled
- Juice of 1 lemon
- 2 tablespoons of vanilla protein powder
- 4 ice cubes, for chilling

Directions

Combine all the smoothie ingredients in a high-speed blender.

Blend all the ingredients by turning on the blender for 2 minutes.

Once the texture is smooth, serve it in tall glasses.

Enjoy.

Nutritional Information

Servings: 3

Amount per serving :

Calories 495

% Daily Value

Total Fat 38.9 g 50%

Saturated Fat 34 g 170%

Cholesterol 9 mg 3%

Sodium 34 mg 1%

Total Carbohydrate 39 g 14%

Dietary Fiber 7.1 g 25%

Total Sugars 23.2 g

Protein 7.2 g

Vitamin D 0 mcg 0%

Calcium 53 mg 4%

Iron 3 mg 18%

Potassium 842 mg 18%

Yellow Mellow Smoothie

This superfood smoothie is a perfect way to boost your mood with the blast of antioxidants. It is a highly nutritious smoothie that provides a burst of energy.

Preparation Time: 5 Minutes

Yield: 2 Servings

Ingredients

- 1 banana

- 1 medium mango, cubed
- ¼ cup cubed pineapple
- 1 teaspoon turmeric
- ½ cup almond milk
- 4 ice cubes
- 1 teaspoon honey
- ½ cup of grapefruit

Directions

Combine all the smoothie ingredients in a high-speed blender.

Pulse all the ingredients at high speed for about 3 minutes.

Once a smooth texture is obtained, pour it into serving glasses and enjoy.

Serve immediately.

Nutritional Information

Servings: 2

Amount per serving:

Calories 334

% Daily Value

Total Fat 15.3 g 20%

Saturated Fat 12.9 g 65%

Cholesterol 0 mg 0%

Sodium 12 mg 1%

Total Carbohydrate 52.9 g 19%

Dietary Fiber 6.7 g 24%

Total Sugars 41.1 g

Protein 4 g

Vitamin D 0 mcg 0%

Calcium 43 mg 3%

Iron 2 mg 11%

Potassium 783 mg 17%

Simple Yellow Smoothie

This smoothie is rich in enzymes that support a healthy gut. It is a very nutritious smoothie that provides instant energy for the body.

Preparation Time: 5 Minutes

Yield: 1–2 Servings

Ingredients

- 2 cups pineapple pieces
- 2 bananas, peeled and frozen
- ½ cup coconut milk

Directions

Place all the smoothie ingredients in a high-speed blender and pulse until smooth.

Pour the smoothie into tall serving glasses and serve.

Enjoy.

Nutritional Information

Servings: 1

Amount per serving:

% Daily Value

Total Fat 29.8 g 38%

Saturated Fat 25.7 g 128%

Cholesterol 0 mg 0%

Sodium 24 mg 1%

Total Carbohydrate 103.9 g 38%

Dietary Fiber 13.4 g 48%

Total Sugars 65.4 g

Protein 7.1 g

Vitamin D 0 mcg 0%

Calcium 73 mg 6%

Iron 4 mg 20%

Potassium 1520 mg 32%

Sunshine Smoothie

This smoothie aids in weight loss and also promotes a healthy gut.

Preparation Time: 10 Minutes

Yield: 2 Servings

Ingredients

- 1 cup Mango chunks

- 1 cup Banana cubes

- 1 cup pineapple juice, fresh

Directions

Blend all ingredients in a high-speed blender.

Once the texture is smooth, serve and enjoy.

Nutritional Information

Servings: 2

Amount per serving:

Calories 183

% Daily Value

Total Fat 0.7 g 1%

Saturated Fat 0.2 g 1%

Cholesterol 0 mg 0%

Sodium 0 mg 0%

Total Carbohydrate 45.6 g 17%

Dietary Fiber 3.5 g 13%

Total Sugars 32.9 g

Protein 2 g

Vitamin D 0 mcg 0%

Calcium 29 mg 2%

Iron 1 mg 4%

Potassium 570 mg 12%

5 GREEN SMOOTHIES

Go Green Smoothie

It is a rich metabolism boosting smoothie, which gives your taste buds a roller coaster ride of flavors. The almond milk adds extra protein to the smoothie, which makes it a high energy boosting drink.

Preparation Time: 8 Minutes

Yield: 2–4 Servings

Ingredients

- 1 orange, peeled and seeded
- ¼ cup strawberries
- 2 cups baby spinach, raw
- 1–2 cups almond milk
- 6 Ice cubes

Directions

Combine all ingredients in a high-speed blender.

Pulse the ingredients until smooth in texture, then serve and enjoy.

Nutritional Information

Servings: 2

Amount per serving :

Calories 319

% Daily Value

Total Fat 28.9 g 37%

Saturated Fat 25.4 g 127%

Cholesterol 0 mg 0%

Sodium 42 mg 2%

Total Carbohydrate 16.8 g 6%

Dietary Fiber 5.2 g 19%

Total Sugars 11.1 g

Protein 4.4 g

Vitamin D 0 mcg 0%

Calcium 78 mg 6%

Iron 3 mg 16%

Potassium 629 mg 13%

Scrub Yourself Smoothie

This smoothie helps clean the toxins from the body and boost the metabolism.

Preparation Time: 6 Minutes

Yield: 2 Servings

Ingredients

- 1/3 cup strawberries

- 1/4 cup pineapple

- 1 cup broccoli florets

- 1 cup kale
- 2 teaspoons honey
- 4 ice cubes, for chilling
- 1 cup almond milk

Directions

Combine all the ingredients in a high- speed blender and pulse until a smooth consistency is obtained.

Pour the smoothie into tall serving glasses and serve.

Enjoy

Nutritional Information

Servings: 2

Amount per serving:

Calories 347

% Daily Value

Total Fat 28.9 g 37%

Saturated Fat 25.4 g 127%

Cholesterol 0 mg 0%

Sodium 4 8mg 2%

Total Carbohydrate 23.5 g 9%

Dietary Fiber 5.1 g 18%

Total Sugars 13.7 g

Protein 5.3 g

Vitamin D 0 mcg 0%

Calcium 93 mg 7%

Iron 3 mg 17%

Potassium 687 mg 15%

Fruit Mix Green Smoothie

This smoothie helps in weight loss and benefits digestion and heart health.

Preparation Time: 10 Minutes

Yield: 2 Servings

Ingredients

- ¼ cup strawberries
- 1 banana
- 2 cups raw spinach
- 1 cup almond milk
- 1 teaspoon vanilla extract

Directions

Put the listed smoothie ingredients in a blender.

Turn on the blender at high speed for two minutes.

Once a smooth texture is obtained, pour the smoothie into ice-filled serving glasses

Serve and enjoy.

Nutritional Information

Servings: 2

Amount per serving :

Calories 347

% Daily Value

Total Fat 29 g 37%

Saturated Fat 25.5 g 127%

Cholesterol 0 mg 0%

Sodium 43 mg 2%

Total Carbohydrate 22.9 g 8%

Dietary Fiber 5.2 g 19%

Total Sugars 12.5 g

Protein 4.4 g

Vitamin D 0 mcg 0%

Calcium 55 mg 4%

Iron 3 mg 17%

Potassium 725 mg 15%

Electric Green Smoothie

It's a rich and scrumptious smoothie that helps fight cancer, heal wounds, and improve immunity. It also includes ingredients that offer better gut health.

Preparation Time: 5 Minutes

Yield: 2 Servings

Ingredients

- ¼ cup pineapple
- 1 orange (peeled and seeded)
- 1 cup raw spinach
- 1 cup kale
- 1½ cups almond milk
- 5 ice cubes, for chilling

Directions

Transfer all the smoothie ingredients to a high-speed blender.

Blend for one minute at high speed.

Once a smooth texture is obtained, pour the smoothie into ice-filled serving glasses.

Serve and enjoy.

Nutritional Information

Servings: 2

Amount per serving:

Calories 349

% Daily Value*

Total Fat 28.8 g 37%

Saturated Fat 25.4 g 127%

Cholesterol 0 mg 0%

Sodium 45 mg 2%

Total Carbohydrate 24.2 g 9%

Dietary Fiber 6 g 21%

Total Sugars 14.7 g

Protein 5.2 g

Vitamin D 0 mcg 0%

Calcium 118 mg 9%

Iron 3 mg 17%

Potassium 753 mg 16%

Apple Pie Smoothie

It is a very filling and low-calorie smoothie that is rich in various antioxidants and cleansing properties. It is a perfect weight loss smoothie to enjoy if you want to shed some extra pounds.

Preparation Time: 10 Minutes

Yield: 2 Servings

Ingredients

- 2 green apples, peeled and cored
- ¼ cup blueberries
- ¼ teaspoon cinnamon
- ¼ teaspoon nutmeg
- 2 cups spinach
- 2 tablespoons chia seeds
- ½ teaspoon vanilla extract
- ½ cup water

Directions

Combine all the mentioned smoothie ingredients in a blender.

Pulse the ingredients for about 2 minutes at high speed.

Once a smooth texture is obtained, pour it into serving glasses and enjoy.

Serve immediately.

Nutritional Information

Servings: 2

Amount per serving:

Calories 207

% Daily Value

Total Fat 5 g 6%

Saturated Fat 0.6 g 3%

Cholesterol 0 mg 0%

Sodium 28 mg 1%

Total Carbohydrate 41 g 15%

Dietary Fiber 11.6 g 41%

Total Sugars 25.4 g

Protein 4 g

Vitamin D 0 mcg 0%

Calcium 124 mg 10%

Iron 3 mg 18%

Potassium 481 mg 10%

5 BLUE SMOOTHIES

Best Blue Smoothie

This smoothie is rich in anti-inflammatory qualities and helps flush toxins from the body.

Preparation Time: 5 Minutes

Yield: 2 Servings

Ingredients

- 8 ounces of coconut milk
- 1 avocado, pitted and scooped from the shell
- 1 banana
- ¼ cup of pineapple chunks
- Sea salt, a pinch
- ½–1 teaspoon blue majik spirulina
- 1 tablespoon of hemp seeds
- ½ cup fresh blueberries

Directions

Combine coconut milk and the avocado in a high-speed blender.

Blend until of a fine consistency.

Then add hemp seeds and blueberries.

Pulse it for 30 seconds.

Next, add all the remaining listed ingredients.

Blend until smoothly combined.

When finished the smoothie becomes homogeneous and has a beautiful blue color.

Pour smoothie into ice-filled glasses and enjoy.

Nutritional Information

Servings: 2

Amount per serving:

Calories 562

% Daily Value

Total Fat 47.7 g 61%

Saturated Fat 28.2 g 141%

Cholesterol 0 mg 0%

Sodium 27 mg 1%

Total Carbohydrate 36.9 g 13%

Dietary Fiber 12 g 43%

Total Sugars 17.2 g

Protein 6.5 g

Vitamin D 0 mcg 0%

Calcium 36 mg 3%

Iron 3 mg 19%

Potassium 1047 mg 22%

Blue Banana Smoothie

It is a perfect glass of smoothie that is rich in nutrients essential for the body and brain. This smoothie is a perfect meal replacement smoothie that keeps the heart healthy and also soothes the digestion.

Preparation Time: 10 Minutes

Yield: 2 Servings

Ingredients

- 2 bananas, peeled and frozen
- 2 small apples, cored and peeled
- ¼ cup of yogurt
- 1 white dragon fruit, (cut the dragon fruit and scoop out the flesh)
- ¼ cup almond milk
- 1 teaspoon blue spirulina powder

Directions

Combine banana, apples, yogurt, dragon fruit, almond milk and blue spirulina powder in a high-speed blender and pulse until smooth.

Pour into ice-filled serving glasses and enjoy.

Nutritional Information

Servings: 2

Amount per serving:

Calories 274

% Daily Value

Total Fat 1.5 g 2%

Saturated Fat 0.5 g 2%

Cholesterol 2 mg 1%

Sodium 49 mg 2%

Total Carbohydrate 67 g 24%

Dietary Fiber 8.5 g 30%

Total Sugars 46.5 g

Protein 3.9 g

Vitamin D 13 mcg 63%

Calcium 63 mg 5%

Iron 1 mg 7%

Potassium 733 mg 16%

Mixed Berries Smoothie

It is a smoothie rich in anti-inflammatory and antioxidant properties.

Preparation Time: 5 Minutes

Yield: 3 Servings

Ingredients

- 1 frozen banana

- 2 tablespoons of veggie vanilla protein powder
- 1 cup almond milk
- 1 cup of blackberries, for topping
- 2 cups blueberries

Directions

Transfer all the smoothie ingredients except the blackberries to a high-speed blender.

Blend it at high speed for about 2 minutes.

Once a smooth texture is obtained, pour it into serving glasses, top with the blackberries and enjoy.

Serve immediately.

Nutritional Information

Servings: 3

Amount per serving:

Calories 330

% Daily Value

Total Fat 20.6 g 26%

Saturated Fat 17.2 g 86%

Cholesterol 23 mg 8%

Sodium 31 mg 1%

Total Carbohydrate 33.4 g 12%

Dietary Fiber 7.7 g 27%

Total Sugars 19.9 g

Protein 8.7 g

Vitamin D 0 mcg 0%

Calcium 51 mg 4%

Iron 3 mg 17%

Potassium 527 mg 11%

Creamy Blue Smoothie

It is a perfect blue smoothie that is full of magnesium, iron, vitamins, and calcium. The smoothie contains antioxidants. It is also rich in zinc and fiber. This smoothie helps reduce the risk of constipation and also reduces the risk of cognitive decline.

Preparation Time: 5 Minutes

Yield: 2 Servings

Ingredients

- 1 pear, cored and chopped
- 2 bananas, peeled
- 6 ounces of blueberries
- 1 teaspoon acai berry powder
- 3 tablespoons cashews
- ½ cup water
- 4 ice cubes, for chilling

Directions

Pulse all the ingredients in a blender.

Once the smoothie is prepared, serve in glasses.

Enjoy.

Nutritional Information

Servings: 2

Amount per serving:

Calories 278

% Daily Value

Total Fat 7.1 g 9%

Saturated Fat 1.4 g 7%

Cholesterol 0 mg 0%

Sodium 0 mg 0%

Total Carbohydrate 55.9 g 20%

Dietary Fiber 8 g 29%

Total Sugars 31.4 g

Protein 4.3 g

Vitamin D 0 mcg 0%

Calcium 21 mg 2%

Iron 2 mg 14%

Potassium 674 mg 14%

Perfect Blue Smoothie

It is a perfect low-calorie smoothie that is rich in antioxidants and low in sugar.

Preparation Time: 5 Minutes

Yield: 3 Servings

Ingredients

- 3 frozen bananas
- 4 tablespoons of hemp seeds
- 2 cups almond milk
- 3 teaspoon blue spirulina powder

Directions

Pulse all the ingredients in a blender.

Once the smoothie is prepared, serve in glasses.

Enjoy.

Nutritional Information

Servings: 3

Amount per serving :

Calories 693

% Daily Value

Total Fat 50.3 g 65%

Saturated Fat 35.8 g 179%

Cholesterol 0 mg 0%

Sodium 416 mg 18%

Total Carbohydrate 46.5 g 17%

Dietary Fiber 8.6 g 31%

Total Sugars 21.1 g

Protein 33 g

Vitamin D 0 mcg 0%

Calcium 85 mg 7%

Iron 16 mg 88%

Potassium 1078 mg 23%

5 LIGHT BLUE SMOOTHIES

Light Blue Smoothie

It is a simple yet classic recipe, which gives a very light blue color once ingredients are blended together. It is a very healthy smoothie that not only boosts the body's stamina but also keeps the digestive system right on track.

Preparation Time: 10 Minutes

Yield: 2 Servings

Ingredients

- 2 bananas, large, frozen
- ½ cup coconut milk
- 1 avocado, pitted and scooped out.
- 2 tablespoons of honey
- ¼ cup of blueberries

Directions

Place all of the mentioned ingredients into your high-speed blender and blend for 2 minutes or till smooth.

Pour into serving glasses and serve immediately.

Nutritional Information

Servings: 2

Amount per serving:

Calories 522

% Daily Value

Total Fat 34.4 g 44%

Saturated Fat 16.9 g 85%

Cholesterol 0 mg 0%

Sodium 17 mg 1%

Total Carbohydrate 58.8 g 21%

Dietary Fiber 11.6 g 41%

Total Sugars 36 g

Protein 4.8 g

Vitamin D 0 mcg 0%

Calcium 29 mg 2%

Iron 2 mg 12%

Potassium 1093 mg 23%

Delicious Smoothie

It is a perfect weight loss and detoxifying smoothie.

Preparation Time: 10 Minutes

Yield: 2 Servings

Ingredients

- ½ head of small red cabbage, chopped
- 2 cups of water
- ½ teaspoon of baking soda
- 2 bananas
- 1 cup coconut milk
- 4 dates, pitted

Directions

Bring the water to a boil in a cooking pot and add the cabbage to it.

Cover the pot and simmer it for 20 minutes.

Then drain the liquid into another pot and save it. Discard the cabbage.

Now reduce 70 percent of the liquid by simmering for 50 minutes.

Next add the baking soda to the liquid, 1/8 teaspoon at a time, stirring.

The liquid will turn light blue.

We will be using the liquid only to add color.

Add together the bananas, dates, and coconut milk in a blender.

Then add only ½ teaspoon of the blue liquid to the blender.

Blend until all ingredients are combined and smooth. Pour smoothie into serving glasses and enjoy.

Nutritional Information

Servings: 2

Amount per serving ;

Calories 485

% Daily Value

Total Fat 29.3 g 38%

Saturated Fat 25.6 g 128%

Cholesterol 0 mg 0%

Sodium 382 mg 17%

Total Carbohydrate 59.2 g 22%

Dietary Fiber 12.7 g 45%

Total Sugars 36.2 g

Protein 7.4 g

Vitamin D 0 mcg 0%

Calcium 129 mg 10%

Iron 4 mg 20%

Potassium 1235 mg 26%

Perfect Light Blue Smoothie

It is a perfect meal replacement smoothie that provides energy and also improves your hair and skin condition.

Preparation Time: 10 Minutes

Yield: 4 Servings

Ingredients

- 1 cup frozen sliced bananas
- 1 tablespoon of coconut oil
- 1 cup coconut cream
- 1 cup almond milk
- Pinch of blue spirulina powder

Directions

Place the ingredients into a high-speed blender and blend for 2 minutes or till smooth.

Pour into ice-filled smoothie glasses and serve chilled.

Nutritional Information

Servings: 4

Amount per serving:

Calories 304

% Daily Value

Total Fat 22.1 g 28%

Saturated Fat 15.9 g 80%

Cholesterol 0 mg 0%

Sodium 293 mg 13%

Total Carbohydrate 23.8g 9%

Dietary Fiber 2.3 g 8%

Total Sugars 14.9 g

Protein 7.2 g

Vitamin D 150 mcg 750%

Calcium 19 mg 1%

Iron 3 mg 17%

Potassium 272 mg 6%

Scrumptious Blue Smoothie

It is a delicious recipe that is packed with nutrients and helps keep hair shiny and also protects against diabetes.

Preparation Time: 10 Minutes

Yield: 2 Servings

Ingredients

- 1/3 cup of blueberries
- 1 cup yogurt
- 1 cup of plain cow's milk

Directions

Blend all ingredients in a high-speed blender.

Once smooth in texture, serve and enjoy.

Nutritional Information

Servings: 2

Amount per serving:

Calories 162

% Daily Value

Total Fat 4.1 g 5%

Saturated Fat 2.7 g 14%

Cholesterol 17 mg 6%

Sodium 143 mg 6%

Total Carbohydrate 18.1 g 7%

Dietary Fiber 0.6 g 2%

Total Sugars 16.5 g

Protein 11.2 g

Vitamin D 1 mcg 3%

Calcium 369 mg 28%

Iron 0 mg 0%

Potassium 375 mg 8%

Blue Banana and Spinach Smoothie

It is a mouth-watering smoothie recipe that does not only taste great but also provides magnesium, iron, and fiber to the body. It is a smoothie that keeps skin healthy, improves eyesight, and also strengthens the muscles.

Preparation Time: 5 Minutes

Yield: 2 Servings

Ingredients

- 2 frozen bananas
- 1/4 teaspoon of blue spirulina
- 1/3 cup spinach
- 1/2 cup of unsweetened almond milk
- 1 tablespoon of shredded coconut
- 1/2 cup sliced almonds
- 1/4 cup organic white mulberries

Directions

Blend all ingredients in a high-speed blender.

Once smooth in texture, serve and enjoy.

Nutritional Information

Servings: 2

Amount per serving:

Calories 279

% Daily Value

Total Fat 14.1 g 18%

Saturated Fat 1.9 g 9%

Cholesterol 0 mg 0%

Sodium 55 mg 2%

Total Carbohydrate 37 g 13%

Dietary Fiber 7.3 g 26%

Total Sugars 17.9 g

Protein 7.3 g

Vitamin D 0 mcg 0%

Calcium 162 mg 12%

Iron 3 mg 14%

Potassium 681 mg 14%

5 PURPLE SMOOTHIES

Purple Power Smoothie

This smoothie is rich in protein and has tons of fiber. It is a perfect energy boosting smoothie with antioxidant quality.

Preparation Time: 10 Minutes

Yield: 2 Servings

Ingredients

- 1 cup raspberries, frozen
- ½ cup blueberries, frozen
- 8 large strawberries, fresh
- 1 cup coconut water
- ¼ cup vanilla Greek yogurt
- 2 tablespoons honey or to taste
- 6 ice cubes, for chilling

Directions

Transfer the entire list of ingredients to a blender and pulse until smooth.

Pour the smoothie into ice-filled serving glasses.

Enjoy.

Nutritional Information

Servings: 2

Amount per serving:

Calories 184

% Daily Value

Total Fat 1.4 g 2%

Saturated Fat 0.4 g 2%

Cholesterol 2 mg 1%

Sodium 135 mg 6%

Total Carbohydrate 42.6 g 15%

Dietary Fiber 7.7 g 27%

Total Sugars 32.4 g

Protein 4.2 g

Vitamin D 0 mcg 0%

Calcium 76 mg 6%

Iron 2 mg 9%

Potassium 574 mg 12%

Purple Punch Smoothie

It is a gut-friendly smoothie with a lot of probiotics and antioxidants.

Preparation Time: 8 Minutes

Yield: 2 Servings

Ingredients

- 1/4 cup yogurt, plain
- 1 cup almond milk
- 1/3 banana, chopped and frozen

- 1/2 cup purple grapes, seedless
- 1/4 cup blueberries
- 1/3 cup blackberries

Directions

Transfer the entire list of ingredients to a blender and pulse until smooth.

Pour the smoothie into ice-filled serving glasses.

Enjoy.

Nutritional Information

- Servings: 2
- Amount per serving:
- Calories 351
- % Daily Value
- Total Fat 29.3 g 38%
- Saturated Fat 25.7 g 129%
- Cholesterol 2 mg 1%
- Sodium 40 mg 2%
- Total Carbohydrate 22.2 g 8%

- Dietary Fiber 5.1 g 18%

- Total Sugars 15.3 g

- Protein 5.3 g

- Vitamin D 0 mcg 0%

- Calcium 87 mg 7%

- Iron 3 mg 14%

- Potassium 554 mg 12%

Detox Purple Smoothie

The perfect blend of vegetables and fruits make it a perfect detox smoothie that helps flush toxins from the body and helps revitalize the skin.

Preparation Time: 10 Minutes

Yield: 4 Servings

Ingredients

- ½ cup raspberries
- 1 cup blackberries
- 1 banana
- 1 cup red cabbage, chopped
- 1 cup red beets, chopped
- 1 cup of baby spinach
- 1 cup Greek yogurt (plain non-fat)
- 1/3 cup orange juice
- 1/2 cup water

Directions

Combine all smoothie ingredients in a blender and blend on high speed until smooth.

Pour the smoothie into ice-filled serving glasses.

Serve cold and enjoy.

Nutritional Information

Servings: 4

Amount per serving:

Calories 311

% Daily Value

Total Fat 6.6 g 8%

Saturated Fat 4.6 g 23%

Cholesterol 15 mg 5%

Sodium 141 mg 6%

Total Carbohydrate 31.8 g 12%

Dietary Fiber 5.2 g 19%

Total Sugars 23.8 g

Protein 32.5 g

Vitamin D 0 mcg 0%

Calcium 340 mg 26%

Iron 1 mg 7%

Potassium 853 mg 18%

Four Ingredients Smoothie

This is a very rich and creamy smoothie recipe that combines astonishing flavors of blueberries, bananas and grape juice. If you want to cleanse the body of toxins, then this smoothie is for you. The addition of yogurt helps to maintain a healthy gut.

Preparation Time: 10 Minutes

Yield: 4 Servings

Ingredients

- 2 cups blueberries
- 2 cups grape juice
- 1 cup plain yogurt
- 2 frozen bananas

Directions

Place all the ingredients into a high-speed blender and pulse until smooth in consistency.

Serve in ice-filled glasses.

Enjoy.

Nutritional Information

Servings: 4

Amount per serving:

Calories 185

% Daily Value

Total Fat 1.3 g 2%

Saturated Fat 0.7 g 4%

Cholesterol 4 mg 1%

Sodium 45 mg 2%

Total Carbohydrate 39.4 g 14%

Dietary Fiber 3.4 g 12%

Total Sugars 29.7 g

Protein 5.3 g

Vitamin D 0 mcg 0%

Calcium 124 mg 10%

Iron 1 mg 8%

Potassium 599 mg 13%

__Purple Smoothie__

Insanely good smoothie, this one is perfect for gut health with a lot of anti-inflammatory properties that reduce inflammation and help cleanse the blood.

Preparation Time: 10 Minutes

Yield: 4 Servings

Ingredients

- 2 bananas, frozen

- ¼ cup of pineapple chunks
- 2 cups of blueberries
- ½ cup soy milk
- ½ cup of cold water
- 1 teaspoon of lemon juice
- 4 ice cubes, for chilling

Directions

Blend all ingredients in a high-speed blender.

Once smooth in texture, serve and enjoy.

Nutritional Information

Servings: 4

Amount per serving :

Calories 116

% Daily Value

Total Fat 1 g 1%

Saturated Fat 0.1 g 1%

Cholesterol 0 mg 0%

Sodium 18 mg 1%

Total Carbohydrate 27.3 g 10%

Dietary Fiber 3.6 g 13%

Total Sugars 16.7 g

Protein 2.3 g

Vitamin D 0 mcg 0%

Calcium 13 mg 1%

Iron 1 mg 8%

Potassium 316 mg 7%

CHAPTER NO- 5

How to Choose the Best Smoothie Blender, and Cups or Bottles

The Best Smoothie Blenders

Making a perfect smoothie is both a very simple and a very complex process. To make a super simple smoothie, you need a blender that is efficient enough to break ice cubes and all the different frozen fruits and vegetables. Usually, blenders come in different capacities and power capabilities. Most blenders have manual blending settings. Choosing the right blender is a very important and crucial decision. Most blenders come in models that range from 200 to 2,000 watts. Fruits and vegetables can easily be blended with the lowest wattage, but the low power makes the blender work hard and shortens its life-span.

If you are a smoothie lover and interested in making thin consistency smoothies, with no hard or frozen ingredients added to it, then buying a blender with a minimum of 600 watts is strongly recommended.

Two factors that are crucial in buying a blender are budget and personal needs. It is not necessary to spend a lot of money on the blender. Price and models become more of a problem if you plan to use this appliance for some other purposes and food preparation, other than just for making smoothies,

High-quality blenders like the Nutri Ninja blending system with smoothie ice-crushing power offer terrific results. If you decided to follow our smoothie cleansing program and want to make some awesome rainbow smoothies, then listed below are some excellent blender recommendations.

Nutri Ninja Pro

This extraordinary Blender can easily break down hard food items.

Magic Bullet Blender

This Magic Bullet Blender is designed for efficient performance.

Cuisinart Portable Blender/Chopper System

This blender can be used for multiple blending with speed and convenience.

Bella Rocket Extract Pro Blender

It is also a very affordable blender that performs highly efficient blending.

PopBabies Blender

These blenders provide a rechargeable base, so you just need to charge it and then you can take it anywhere you want. It is a best friend to all the travelers and the people who are on the move. And it doesn't take up much space either.

The Best Smoothie Cups or Bottles

After choosing a blender to make very delicious rainbow smoothies, now it's time to choose the best quality cups, bottles, and containers in which to enjoy the smoothie or even take it out of the house to school or to the office.

Listed below are some highly recommended smoothie cups and bottles, which you may want to purchase.

Blender Bottle with Wire Ball (Large 28 Oz)

This blender bottle holds about 28 ounces of liquid and is perfect for holding a large amount of smoothie. This kind of bottle has a wire ball inside that is able to shake up your smoothie. It works very well with the powders that are added to some smoothies and need to be whisked. It can shake thickened smoothies very well. The bottle does not spill any liquid from the top.

The look of the bottle is very catchy. The design is slim, and the opening for drinking the smoothie is very nice and wide, so thick smoothies easily flow out. These bottles are dishwasher safe. They don't have handles.

Clear Glass Water Bottles

These bottles are perfect for storing smoothies and beverages. The design is cylindrical, and the upper part is quite wide, so drinking and pouring the smoothie becomes easy. The lid offers a tight fit that keeps the smoothie fresh and does not allow any spillage. It is easy to add additional items to the bottle. These bottles are dishwasher safe. They are made from very thick plastic. It is a great bottle to hold smoothies, protein shakes, nut milk, lemonade, and water. Also, they easily fit in the car cup holders.

Bubba 52 ounces Travel Mug

These travel mugs came in different sizes to suit your daily needs. The design of the mug has dual wall insulation, which keeps the cold food cold up to 12 hours and hot food hot for 3 hours. If you want to take a large amount of smoothies with you, then these mugs are perfect for you. The drinking opening is large enough for a smoothie to go through. There is an air hole that is always open to let steam escape and to equilibrate the pressure.

Thermos Hydro Active Sports Bottle, 15 Ounces

These Water bottles are great for smoothies. These bottles have removable ice tubs which keep your drink cool. The design is pretty, and it is easy to drink the smoothie due to the rapid flow design. It is very light and easy to hold. The top is very easy to open and close, and it also feels very secure. It doesn't seem to spill. One of the drawbacks of these bottles is that they cannot hold a large amount of smoothie because of their small size. It only holds one serving of smoothie.

Camelbak Better Bottle

Available in different varieties and sizes, these bottles are like Sippy cups for adults. The lid opens quickly, and the bottle is usually very easy to clean. The models come in a variety of colors and are very easy to use.

Loop Cap and Cafe Cap Brushed Stainless Steel Bottles: 12 Ounces

These bottles are made from stainless steel. They are not the biggest bottles available on the market. The design is slim, and they are very comfortable to hold and can be carried without any fear of spillage.

Conclusion

This smoothie book contains all those recipes which will help you to achieve your diet goals. Now being able to control illness or inflammation and to lose excess weight is not such a complex process.

If you are a person who has medical problems and becomes frustrated by just thinking of all the diet plans that never seem to work for you, then replace your meals with our healthy, rich, mouth-watering, and nutritional smoothies. They will not only make you feel contented, but will also make you feel satisfied, and will keep your cravings at bay.

The cleansing program introduced in this book helps you to change your life and helps your body to perform its functions more effectively and efficiently.

Hopefully, this comprehensive book will make you feel much healthier and happier.

Remember, it is very important to consult with your physician or health care provider before using the 7-day smoothie cleansing diet.

Made in the USA
Columbia, SC
25 April 2019